TEACHERS

Written By:
Herbert I. Kavet

Illustrated By:
Martin Riskin

Many thanks to my Research Assistant, Alex Loria,
without whose help the factual content of this book
would have been even less.

Ivory Tower Publishing Co., Inc.
125 Walnut Street
P.O. Box 9132
Watertown, MA 02272-9132
Telephone #: (617) 923-1111   Fax #: (617) 923-8839

Introduction

Yes, I taught for a few years, but I won't tell you where or when, fearing derision and disbelief from you REAL teachers. Besides, I can say almost anything in an introduction 'cause no one ever reads introductions. Chances are, you got this book as a gift, probably the idea of a student's parent, either in gratitude or as a bribe, so there's little chance you can return it no matter how I lie. You'll find all my sources and a list of research associates in the bibliography at the end of the book, unless I forget.

The Bladder of a Camel

Most people don't realize how traumatic it is for a teacher to maintain normal toilet habits. The kids raise their hands, get a pass and go merrily off to do their business or create mayhem in the rest rooms, as the case may be. The kids can slip into the boys' or girls' room between classes while the teacher sternly stands hall duty. Lunch offers another opportunity for the kids, while the teacher, as lunchroom guard, risks disaster by even blinking, much less disappearing for a minute or two. Is it any wonder teachers develop the bladder of a camel to carry them through?

Vacations

The only time you can take a vacation, of course, all your students are off, too, and it takes a clever teacher to avoid running into them. One sure-fire method, if you can stand it, is to concentrate your visits to educational attractions. "Oh, yes, we spent the summer at the Philbert Pen & Pencil Museum in Sandusky, Ohio—really fascinating and we learned so much." Teachers' children rarely get to visit Disneyland, and when they do, so many other kids are on vacation, the lines are too long to get into anything.

"MRS. MERTLINGER, MRS. MERTLINGER, MARYBETH PUSHED ME!"

Summer Vacation

People who don't teach are so envious of our summers and other vacations. They fail to realize that teachers, usually living in poverty, can't afford to spend their vacations touring mountains in Italy or Norwegian Fjords. Teaching summer school is not much of a change, but it's much less humiliating than competing with your students for lawn mowing jobs.

"OH NO, WE HAD TO SEE THE REAL MEXICO."

"IF YOU DON'T QUIET DOWN, I'M GOING TO HAVE TO CALL IN THE NEW SUBSTITUTE ASSISTANT."

Classroom Rumors

The kids spend hours a day staring at their teachers and, provided they are awake, they become incredibly observant of any changes in your dress or manner. My wife taught math at a Junior High and during her first year of teaching, tried to be nice and friendly to her students. Her next year found her much less tolerant of nonsense and she ran a much stricter classroom. She also happened to have married me over that summer and the rumor going around school was that I beat her, which caused her to become so mean.

The rumor that Ms. Riley gave her last "A" in 1961
lent a sober air to her classes.

Classroom Rumors

Kids will grab onto any fragment to generate a rumor. They should only have such imagination in a creative writing class. Heaven forbid your fly is unzipped or the third button on your blouse left undone or you'll be blessed (or cursed) with the reputation as a sex maniac for the rest of your career at that school.

Word of Ms. Lollinger's new blouse spread quickly.

What the Kids Really Think

1. You are very, very old.

2. You'll remember them forever.

3. Your whole life revolves around teaching.

4. When you fail to return graded papers, it's because you are reading them so carefully.

5. You get angry when school is closed for weather emergencies.

TEACHER   VICE PRINCIPAL   SUBSTITUTE   PRINCIPAL

"DR. LEMAY SUGGESTED THAT YOU TRY MOTIVATING YOUR STUDENTS BEFORE SENDING THEM TO HIS OFFICE."

Bad Days

You just know it's going to be a bad day when...

1. The Principal sits in on a class.

2. The kids all drop their pencils at exactly 9:37 a.m.

3. The Guidance Counselor sets up a parent conference on Friday afternoon.

4. The nurse's office can't find your class's immunization records.

5. You have lunchroom duty on a day when they're serving watermelon for dessert.

Phone Calls

Most working adults can receive or make an occasional phone call during the day. Emergencies arise, hair appointments must be cancelled, insurance claims called in and of course, you'll want to talk to your service manager to authorize an $875 car repair, just to give a few examples. Teachers can almost never receive calls and can only make them with the office clerks and assistant principal eavesdropping and hanging on every word. It's even more frustrating if you teach in a wealthy school district where half the kids have pagers and cellular phones.

"WHEN HE HUNCHES OVER LIKE THAT, HE'S TELLING HER HE LOVES HER."

The Parent/Teacher Conference

1. "Jason is bored in class."

2. "Her friends are a bad influence."

3. "She never acts that way at home."

4. "Billy says he never has homework."

5. "How can you let them outside in weather like this!?"

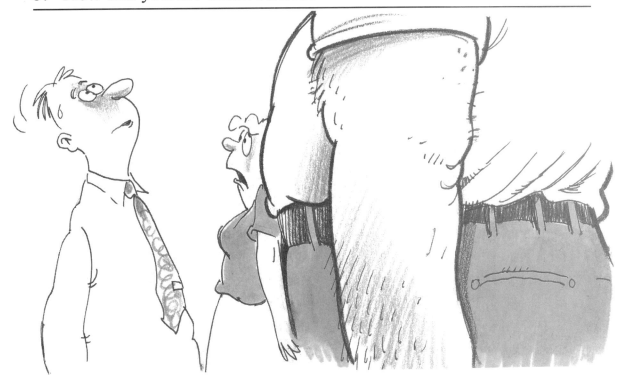

"THE REASON SCOTT IS ALWAYS FIGHTING, IS THAT THE OTHER BOYS PICK ON HIM."

Kids Who Are Smarter Than Their Teacher

Sometimes the kid is a genius. Sometimes you're a little unprepared and sometimes you just can't answer a really good question. What to do?

1. Admit it.
2. Fudge it.
3. Ignore it.

When you fudge it, offering the question as an extra credit homework assignment is always a good ploy.

Administration and Teaching

Late slips, detention forms, class registers, plan books, attendance reports, permission slips and health documents, just to mention a few, can really occupy your entire school day. This makes the school administration happy, but leaves dedicated teachers with a vague uneasy feeling of unfulfillment regarding teaching. The kids, of course, couldn't care less one way or the other. They're too busy with who got her or his ear pierced, who was caught making out behind the gym and why only 26 people can be on the Varsity Traveling Team. You can ignore most of the administrative baloney and it probably will go away. Most forms were developed, after all, by well-intentioned idiots to cover their butts.

"...AND THIS FORM REMINDS YOU TO GET THE REGISTER FORM BACK ON TIME."

"MRS. FITZBERGER, PLEASE COME DOWN — WE WON'T PUT JASON BACK IN YOUR CLASS."

Every Teacher is an Author

Every teacher dreams of publishing a book and using it as a catapult to fame and fortune. And they all can do it, too—look at this book. Most of the teachers in the country could write a much funnier book, probably with fewer grammatical errors. (Then again, they don't own the Publishing Company which publishes this nonsense, like I do.) Confidentially, without a spell check feature on my computer, I'd never have the courage to publish a book meant to be read by teachers. For all I know, Miss Riley is still teaching out there and just waiting for an excuse to put me back into 4th grade.

"THESE PARENT'S NIGHTS MAKE YOU APPRECIATE THE INTELLIGENCE OF YOUR KIDS A LOT MORE."

Back-to-School Nights

In addition to being nervous about talking in front of this group of taxpayers, you have the problem of explaining that the grades are made up of 1/3 tests, 2/5 papers, 1/6 class participation, 1/4 homework and 17/64 final exam, to a group who never learned fractions any better than you did. Back-to-school nights are made tolerable by the attendance of all those concerned parents whom you don't really need to see or explain things to. The ones you really want to see are not there, and you can only picture them guzzling beer or creating mayhem at the local pool hall.

"YOUR WHOLE YEAR WILL BE EASIER IF YOU TRAIN THE PARENTS AT THE FIRST BACK-TO-SCHOOL NIGHT."

Teacher/Parent Conferences

The tough part about meeting the parents is associating their name with the kid's face. This is made much tougher with the mix and match propensity that accompanies divorce. Once that is accomplished, you can use any of the following explanations to politely describe their darling's behavior:

What you say:	**What you really mean:**
He's very active.	Smashed 2 desks and a window during the first week.
Doesn't work to capacity.	He's failing everything and we only promoted him because he's terrorizing the children who are 5 years younger.
Sometimes fails to concentrate.	She looks at boys all day and we catch her making out in study hall 3 times a week.

Teacher/Parent Conferences

What you say:	What you really mean:
Needs to be motivated.	Combs her hair all day.
Easily distracted.	Mostly he looks at his watch lest he be slow in leaving his desk at the first bbbring of the bell.
Limited attention span.	Waits for bell only when not gazing out window.

Book Covers

Your pupils probably figure that teachers hold some sort of book cover concession from which they derive incredibly valuable benefits like summer trips to Europe or cents-off coupons for chocolate milk. Why else, they reason, would there be this fanatical obsession with book covers? Other than the satisfaction of recycling brown paper bags, we all know there is little benefit derived from covering books other than giving the kids a surface to doodle on. The insides are torn to pieces or obsolete long before the covers wear out.

"SANDY IS ALWAYS COMPLAINING HOW BROKE SHE IS."

Every Teacher Has Their "Thing"

With some, it's punctuality. Papers and homework must be in on time—no extensions. It teaches responsibility. Others are into creativity. Do a term paper in bubble gum and the creative teacher is in ecstasy. And there are many others: no crossing out—get it right the first time; neatness counts; group projects teach teamwork; class participation; learn to express yourself.

It's the students' job to figure out the teacher's "thing" each year. Once they do, a happy teacher and a fine grade is assured.

"MR. PENWELLER HAS A THING ABOUT GERMS."

Jan finally found the missing exams from 1989.

Pedagogy

Teaching is easy. Man, yes, even animals, have been teaching their young ever since little corpuscles crawled out of the primeval kitchen years ago and life began at suburban malls. What's hard, is understanding all the new terminology that is tossed at teachers each year: shared leaders, awareness concepts, cooperative learners, dynamic management, educated growth. Real teachers have no idea what these terms mean. It's hard enough remembering the kids' names and all the administration procedures, not to mention losing your lesson plans in the back seat of your car.

"AND WHAT ABOUT THE TIME IN 1982 WHEN YOU DIDN'T GIVE BACK THE MATH EXAM?"

April Fools' Day

Dreaded April Fools' Day requires an extra level of alertness from teachers. Preparation starts the evening before, ensuring all articles of clothing to be worn that day are flawless. Care must be exercised at the mirror after each meal, to make sure poppy seeds or spinach aren't caught in your teeth or strands of something aren't hanging from your hair. In Japan, it's called FU KOOMBOWA ITCHIBIDDY Day, which means literally, "There's tofu dangling from your nose."

Teachers' Union

Most teachers have a vague uneasy feeling about "The Union," as though it's sort of a necessary but slightly undignified blue collar institution. Unions are necessary, of course. For all their cries for top level education for their kids, taxpayers are a cheap lot who would much rather visit Mexico or redo the bathroom than pay their children's teachers a living wage. Putting in a new football stadium is also an entirely different matter.

"THE VIOLENCE AT THESE TEACHER STRIKES IS LIMITED TO POKING WITH AN ERASER."

Teachers' Stress

Teachers' stress is defined as "the confusion created by your mind when it overrides the body's basic desire to choke the living daylights out of some idiot who desperately deserves it." You resist this desire for physical action because the superintendent, foolishly, doesn't allow corporal punishment anymore, and because usually the parents are more to blame than the kids, and they are often bigger than you.

"MRS. TATTLEBAUM..., MRS. TATTLEBAUM..., WE'RE SORRY!"

Anger Management

When you have an unmitigated urge to kill a student, it's best to close your eyes, count slowly to 10 and then give a pop quiz, should anyone be remaining in the classroom.

Time Management

New teachers always worry about preparing enough material to last the class hour. After the first few months, this former worry is a source of great amusement. It's obvious that getting through even a small fraction of whatever you prepared is totally impossible. "Today we're going to examine the word 'THE.'" But, first the attendance report, 4 late slips, an announcement from the administration office, a memo for everyone to sign from the nurse, 4 questions on if it'll be on the test, 2 questions on what the homework assignment will be, a flurry of desperate pleas for the rest room pass and oops, there's the bell.

Each term, Mrs. Gallagher was able to find one kid who enabled her to make the department head think she was computer literate.

Handling Disruptive Students

1. Insist they act their age (Then send them to detention when they do).

2. Set fair but firm and definite rules and then stick to them (Be sure to stay flexible for specific situations).

3. Don't be afraid to ask for help from the school administrators and counselors (Then have the Union mediate your terrible evaluation for not being able to control your class).

The Gifted Child's Parent

A gifted child is a delight to have in your class. The thirst for knowledge and the quick grasp of this student, after all, is why you went into teaching in the first place. The gifted child's parents, however, are worse than any two class pests. These parents want to talk to you each week, sometimes with Grandma or an aunt   in tow, ostensibly to check if their genius is bored or being continuously stimulated, but really to hear how smart their child is. Give them the praise in 30 second capsules and immediately suggest some extra credit homework or you'll never get to the supermarket.

Teachers at Parties

Ever notice how squirmy people get at parties when they hear you are a teacher? It's like they are afraid to make some sort of grammatical error in their conversation or you're going to ask them to prove the Pythagorean Theorem. Casual acquaintances will never talk about sex or money in your presence, cutting out 90% of their conversational repertoire, and in truth, the only people who gravitate to you are parents of kids you have in your classes who have a vested interest in buttering you up.

Teachers at Parties

Parents, when they find out you are a teacher, always think you'd like to hear about their kid. It would be OK if they had a question or two to ask you, but they are only interested in boring you with how little Jason wasn't stimulated at the public schools but blossomed with the dedicated teachers at Brooksfield Academy. They will lull you to sleep with how the guidance counselors thought Melissa should go to an Ivy League School, but she selected Milford State because of its superb pre-veterinary program.

"WE'RE UNDER TERRIFIC PRESSURE TO HAVE OUR STUDENTS DO WELL ON THE STANDARDIZED TEST."

Professional Days

Many school systems, instead of paying you a professional salary, will throw you a few professional days every year with which you should do something professional. Sleeping in is nice, as is doing research on your tan at a beach. Professional conferences are a very legitimate use of this time, especially if held in Atlantic City or Las Vegas.

"THESE CONFERENCES GIVE YOU AN OPPORTUNITY TO ACT JUST LIKE YOUR STUDENTS."

The Crux of Teaching

Getting up in the dark on cold, winter mornings in order to drive to school while juggling a coffee cup between your knees, so you can punch in before the warning bell, which then enables you to have a few moments to erase the obscenities from the blackboard.

Teachers' Parking Lot

Don't look for BMW's, year-old Mercedes or classy Japanese luxury cars here. What you'll find are 1969 VW's, 1973 Caprices, Honda Civics and late model, heavily financed Ford Escorts, all with back seats filled with a collection of donut wrappings, coffee cups, crumbling class projects and missing homework papers, not to mention 300,000 rubber bands and enough paper clips to equal the steel output of medium sized third world countries.

If school systems could somehow shift this back seat treasure trove from teachers' cars to the school supply room, teachers would never again have to spend their own money for school supplies, and thousands of kids would finally have their homework papers returned.

Teachers' Cars

We've already discussed the hazardous waste disaster area that passes for the insides and more particularly the back seats of teachers' cars. The exterior is usually worse. Generations of students have taken out their frustrations over grades and school on the surface of teachers' cars. They do terrible things to the paint job, which in many cases is all there is available to hold the rust together, and they play mischievous games with the air valves and tires. The scene where kids in the shop class restore a teacher's car to a shiny treasure only happens in the movies.

The Informer

Every teacher needs an informer to keep them apprised about what really is going on in the class. The lines of communication with this little squealer enable even inexperienced teachers to develop a reputation of having eyes in the back of their heads and the uncanny ability to know who is copying homework from whom. The time to draw the line on this despicable practice is when you start getting information on what Luke and Jennifer did in the back of the bus and details on last weekend's mailbox smashing adventure.

Paperwork

Schools are oiled with paperwork. They run on registers, roll books, seating plans, lesson plans, memos, circulars, directives, not to mention slips—excuse slips, late slips, library slips and that's just for the morning home room. This avalanche of paper descends on the poor teacher who could never even get through a Book of the Month Club commitment. What teacher can pass up 12 books for only $4 plus postage which (and it makes you wonder why the post office is always broke), somehow comes to $137.40. I don't know how we got on this, but it's cheaper to use the library.

"GIVE THEM BROKEN COPIERS AND HIDE THEIR BELL SCHEDULES."

The Teachers' Lounge

This is how the kids picture the teachers' lounge. In actuality the jacuzzi tends to be crowded, the decor is often dated, the air conditioning occasionally proves inadequate and the teachers are always at odds over the volume of the background music.

Regarding the gossip and rumors generated in this room, they are worse than anything the students can imagine.

This is how the kids picture the teachers' lounge.

Time for Grading Papers

Time management for teachers means grading papers. Experienced teachers never spend time on lesson plans once they're finished student teaching in college. Grading papers is where the pressure on your home life comes from, and the duty must be carefully managed.

When it came time to move, Mrs. Finkelstein had to figure out what to do with 22 years of homework, projects, pop quizzes and papers that she never quite got around to grading.

5 Methods for Grading Papers

1. Wait until the pile of papers threatens to avalanche and destroy the structural integrity of your house.

2. Wait until the kids' asking for their paper back occupies more time than teaching.

3. Always grade all the papers the same day you receive them. This method proved very effective for the one teacher in Wisconsin who tried it.

4. Have the students grade each other's papers and then hope the principal doesn't catch you.

5. Wait for the weekend and then don't do it.

Control of Your Class

Studies have shown that nothing works better than a tattoo. This is for male or female teachers, and dragons and knives are better than hearts and flowers—you want to be known as a fighter with a possibly violent past, not as a lover. If for some reason you don't take the tattoo approach or can't manage to show enough of it to gain respect, the only other way to keep control of a class is through REPUTATION. Once a teacher gets a reputation as a tough cookie, managing a class is child's play. Don't ask me how. I don't know either.

Former Students

You see them at the mall or they become your dentist or you read a notice that they've opened a law office in town. You remember their names and how they used to be such an itch and usually, if you meet them, they remember you or at least pretend. Every now and then you get a touching note with a confession about how you affected a young life and all the grief about being a teacher becomes worthwhile.

These other books are available at many fine stores.

#2350 Sailing. Using the head at night • Sex & Sailing • Monsters in the Ice Chest • How to look nautical in bars and much more nautical nonsense.

#2351 Computers. Where computers really are made • How to understand computer manuals without reading them • Sell your old $2,000,000 computer for $60 • Why computers are always lonely and much more solid state computer humor.

#2352 Cats. Living with cat hair • The advantages of kitty litter • Cats that fart • How to tell if you've got a fat cat.

#2353 Tennis. Where do lost balls go • Winning the psychological game • Catching your breath • Perfecting wood shots.

#2354 Bowling. A book of bowling cartoons that covers: Score sheet cheaters • Boozers • Women who show off • Facing your team after a bad box and much more.

#2355 Parenting. Understanding the Tooth Fairy • 1000 ways to toilet train • Informers and tattle tales • Differences between little girls and little boys • And enough other information and laughs to make every parent wet their beds.

#2356 Fitness. T-shirts that will stop them from laughing at you • Earn big money with muscles • Sex and Fitness • Lose weight with laughter from this book.

#2357 Golf. Playing the psychological game • Going to the toilet in the rough • How to tell a real golfer • Some of the best golf cartoons ever printed.

#2358 Fishing. Handling 9" mosquitoes • Raising worms in your microwave oven • Neighborhood targets for fly casting practice • How to get on a first name basis with the Coast Guard plus even more.

#2359 Bathrooms. Why people love their bathroom • Great games to help pass the time on toilets • A frank discussion of bathroom odors • Plus lots of other stuff everyone out of diapers should know.

#2360 Biking. Why the wind is always against you • Why bike clothes are so tight • And lots of other stuff about what goes thunk, thunk, thunk when you pedal.

#2361 Running. How to "go" in the woods • Why running shoes cost more than sneakers • Keeping your lungs from bursting by letting the other guy talk.

#2362 Skiing. Understanding ski reports • Chair lift etiquette • Why trail maps don't show trees • Where moguls really come from • Rules for hot tubs and saunas

#2363 Doctors. Handling lawyer and insurance problems with a rusty scalpel • Offshore medical schools and conferences • Why surgeons always get to carve the turkey on Thanksgiving • And a lot more humor that can be easily digested between patients.

#2364 Lawyers. Making faces at the judge • Why lawyers make better lovers • Quit law and make more money as a plumber • The first lawyer book ever written with more jokes for lawyers than about them.

#2365 Teachers. How teachers develop the Bladder of a Camel • Handling Back-to-School Nights and April Fools' Day • Recruiting an informer • Out-smarting kids who are smarter than you.

#2366 Nurses. Making the doctor look good • Ways to eject obnoxious visitors • Why nurses never get sick • Making big money in nursing • Great presents patients give you.

Ivory Tower Publishing Co., Inc.   125 Walnut St., PO Box 9132, Watertown, MA 02272-91
Telephone #: (617) 923-1111   Fax #: (617) 923-8839